King David

THE

THRESHOLD

BETWEEN

TWO AGES

Lilly Funk

PUBLISHING

Published by

Open Doors Publishing
629 Bayridge Blvd
Willowick, OH 44095
austin.funk23@gmail.com

Printed in the United States of America

First Printing

ISBN: 9798334567917

Table of Contents

Introduction

Have you ever pictured King David as a frail old king? What would you imagine? Would you picture him with a long gray beard? Would he move about slowly, pacing the walls of his house, looking over the kingdom he had ruled for many long years, the place he experienced glory and treachery, the depths of sorrow and utmost joy? What would he think about? What motivations would he have, what priorities? What would he care about most as his days on earth came to a close?

A few years ago, whenever I thought of David from the Old Testament, I thought of a young shepherd boy watching over his flock at night and defending it from lions. Or I thought of a little underdog facing off against the bully Goliath. Sometimes I even thought of a young man in exile fleeing a jealous King Saul, or of a middle-aged king committing adultery and then murder to try to cover it up. But I rarely thought of an old king at the close of his reign.

I also thought David was so overrated. He was the "perfect child" of the Bible; he shone like an angel in comparison with King Saul; he was mentioned constantly by prophets, the writers of the New Testament, and by Jesus Himself; even when he did fall and make mistakes, those mistakes were just textbook.

It wasn't until I personally studied David's life that he came alive to me as a person with depth of character and depth of heart. Especially in his later life, when he faced the end rather than the promise of a fruitful reign, his actions and words revealed the kind of person he had become, a person who often filled my eyes with tears and my heart with regard. King David is now a person I can't help but respect and hold dear, and who now comes closer in my estimation to matching that praise of being "after [God's] own heart"[1] and that honor of Jesus Himself being called "the Son of David."[2]

The picture of David's character that especially jumped out at me, the picture I'd like to try to paint through this book, is that old, gray-haired king. That old man stood at the turning point of something marvelous between God and His people. As David closed out his reign and passed away from the face of the earth, an entire age ended and another began. The age that ended was an age of God

---

1. Acts 13:22 NKJV

2. Matt. 1:1

2

dwelling with His people in the tabernacle—a movable, transient tent. And the age that began was an age of God dwelling with His people in the temple—a permanent, established building. David's later life and reign was at the threshold between these two ages. Something about him and his love for God incited this end of *the tent* and the beginning of *the building*.

The Tabernacle and the Temple

In my studies on King David, I read the works of a number of Bible scholars who wrote on the differences between the tabernacle and the temple. I will present some of what I read as well as my own thoughts and conclusions in order to introduce the tabernacle and temple, these two ways that God dwelt with His people.

Hundreds of years before David was born, God's people wandered the wilderness, carrying as they went the ark of God, on which God dwelt "between the cherubim."[3] Whenever God's people stopped to set up camp, they put a tent over the ark and surrounded the tent with a wall of fabric. This tented dwelling place for God was "movable and provisional" and "did not represent an established or permanent order of things."[4] At that time, it made sense for God to dwell in a movable setup because His people had to move about. But still, how strange it was for the God of the universe to settle into a

---

3. 1 Sam. 4:4

4. Coates, *The House of God*, 46.

mere tent. Imagine if the president of the United States lived in an RV. It doesn't match. There is a reason that the White House was built.

Yet, God dwelt with His people in this "movable and provisional" way until, at last, they came to the promised land, where they set up the tent more permanently. But then, at a time when the people had barely gotten their footing as a nation, they lost the ark of God in a battle with their enemies.

David was born in the midst of this confusion. When he became king, the first part of his reign was filled with establishing the kingdom, defeating enemy nations, and preparing a place for the ark in Jerusalem. This majority of his reign matched in character the age of the tabernacle, being regarded as a time of "change, conflict, and trial."[5] Just like the nation of Israel was not yet fully established, God's dwelling place among His people was also not yet fully established on the earth.

When the temple was built under Solomon, it brought with it the thought of permanence, grandness, and rest. By the time David's reign was over, "the Lord [had] put his foes under the soles of his feet."[6] After this victory over other nations had been established, under Solomon the Lord gave "rest on every side; there [was] neither adversary nor evil occurrence."[7]

5. A. B. Simpson, *The Christ in the Bible Commentary, Volume Two*, 361.

6. 1 Kings 5:3

7. 1 Kings 5:4

The age of the temple was secure, peaceful, and prosperous. The wisdom of Solomon and the wealth of the kingdom were known even in other lands.[8] The temple itself was a tangible, visible manifestation of the glory of God among His people. And at last, God was dwelling in a place that matched His character.

If the things written in the Old Testament were "a shadow of things to come"[9] and were meant to become "our examples,"[10] what can we learn from the ages of the tabernacle and the temple? The church today, without a permanent home or exalted status on the earth, is like God's people carrying around the tabernacle. And the day we are looking forward to, when the church will shine in glory with her King, will be like Solomon's kingdom where the glory of God will be known throughout the earth. Thus, looking at the tabernacle age as a picture of the church today and the temple age as a picture of the church after Christ returns, we can see how King David fits in the middle of them as an example for us who are also waiting for that day when the glory of God is established throughout the earth in reality.

But before we talk about David, I want to mention a few points I found valuable when comparing the tabernacle and the church today. If you imagine the tabernacle based on its description in Exodus, two

---

8. 2 Chron. 9:5. "Then she said to the king: 'It was a true report which I heard in my own land about your words and your wisdom.'"

9. Col. 2:17

10. 1 Cor. 10:6

5

things jump out regarding its physical appearance. The first is that it was clearly mobile, indicated by the rings on the sides of every piece of furniture through which to insert poles for carrying. The church today is only wandering on the earth. We have our true home in Christ, but our position on the earth is a temporary one. The Apostle Paul talks of our bodies as "our earthly house [or] tent" and that "we groan, earnestly desiring to be clothed with our habitation which is from heaven."[11] There is something permanent that we are waiting for which we do not yet have. Just like God's people sojourned with the tabernacle through the wilderness, the church today is sojourning in the world without a permanent resting place.

The second aspect of its physical appearance worth noting is that the tabernacle was not that impressive from the outside. If you were a visitor to the Israelite camp and came up to the tabernacle, you would see the outer wall made of white linen and beyond that wall, sticking up in the center, a big bulge of a tent covered in badger skin.[12] The tent would not be covered in velvet or silk cloth, not even sheep's wool. It would be covered in a plain brown skin. However, if you walked into the tent, inside you would see a room full of gold—walls covered in gold,[13] a lampstand beaten out of pure gold,[14] a showbread

---

11. 2 Cor. 5:1–2

12. Exod. 26:14. "You shall also make a covering of ram skins dyed red for the tent, and a covering of badger skins above that."

13. Exod. 26:15, 29

14. Exod. 25:31

table overlaid with gold,[15] and an incense altar overlaid with gold.[16] Then in the deepest room of the tent would be the ark of God overlaid with gold.[17]

The church today is composed of average people. It doesn't physically shine with the glory of God. It is not at the forefront of monarchies or governments. Buried inside the cord of lauded human history is a little thread of people who loved the Lord Jesus, often misunderstood in their generations. Just like there was not yet a building to be seen and admired by other nations, "at the present moment the kingdom [of God] is not set up in public manifestation."[18]

However, the church is golden on the inside. We are as of yet only earthen vessels which contain great treasure inside.[19] But what a treasure we have, God Himself dwelling in us and waiting for the day He will be fully glorified through us, when the church will come out of its struggling, wandering tabernacle age and come into an age where it will become like Solomon's temple, displayed throughout the world as the glory of God established on the earth.

15. Exod. 25:23–24

16. Exod. 30:1–3

17. Exod. 25:10–11

18. Coates, *The House of God*, 47.

19. 2 Cor. 4:7

David and Solomon

Not only do the characteristics of the tabernacle and temple tell us about these two ages, but their kings do too. David and Solomon each represent Christ in different stages of His ministry. David represents Christ learning obedience as a man and being perfected in suffering until He, too, as foreshadowed by David, "put all our spiritual enemies under the soles of His feet, so that we may have 'rest on every side.'"[20] Solomon represents Christ in "the day of His glory,"[21] enjoyed after the victory won in the previous age. Christ "is the true David and the true Solomon," "the Man of war and the Man of rest and peace."[22] And because Solomon was anointed king while David was still alive, "both were on the throne at the same time, mak[ing] it much easier to understand the type of Christ in this. It is one person, whom His sufferings and victories place on the throne of glory and of peace."[23]

The temple is a result both of Christ as "the true David who…has put every foe beneath His feet" and of Christ as "the true Solomon in the blessed rest and peace of resurrection."[24] We can know the reality of these truths, "can enter in by faith and in the Spirit,"[25] even though

---

20. Coates, *The House of God*, 47.

21. Coates, 47.

22. Coates, 49–50.

23. Darby, *Synopsis of the Bible*.

24. Coates, 50.

25. Coates, 50.

we do not see them completely realized. It is wonderful to know that our Lord has secured victory and rest for us, and even more wonderful to know that the victory and rest will one day be worked out in full on the earth. We are able today to experience Him in both of these attributes—as the conquering Lord (David) and as the restful King (Solomon)—knowing that "in a quickly coming day they will be publicly displayed in power and glory."[26]

At the end of David's life, he drew up plans for the temple, gathered materials for it, determined the location for its build, and made other preparations that led up to the actual building of the temple. If David represents Christ securing the land for God's people, then his preparations for the temple seem to represent Christ building His church. But I don't want to look at David's life in a way where I can just sit back and watch Christ as He does it all. It is hard for me to say that I am not also involved in building His church. The Bible says that Jesus will build His church,[27] and it also says that the church builds itself up in love.[28] "For this house is built both by us…and by God."[29] How can I learn from David—his character, his preparations, his heart, and his actions—to become someone who can prepare God's dwelling place and usher in that coming age?

26. Coates, 50.

27. Matt. 16:18

28. Eph. 4:16

29. Augustine, *City of God,* trans. Marcus Dods, 520.

"It was reserved to Solomon to build the house, but David was the one who secured the place for it, and who provided the material."[30] The kingdom will surely be complete and glorious one day, but it is the work of us *today* to gather the materials and prepare everything for the building. So how exactly did David facilitate this transition from the age of the tabernacle to the age of the temple? What can we learn from him to become people who can bring Christ back and give God a permanent, glorious dwelling on the earth? This book will attempt to answer those questions.

---

30. Coates, *The House of God*, 50.

How God Dwelt with His People before David's Time

Before David had his dream of building a house for God, God had a number of ways in which He was with His people. At first, He only walked with a few of them. Then He spoke to a nation of them from a mountain. Then He dwelt with that nation in a tent. My goal in this section is to look at these stages of God dwelling with His people and what hurdles had to be overcome in order for God to dwell with them in that way. The stories that I pull out will not exhaust every instance where God dwelling with His people is mentioned. But these are parts that stood out to me. At the end of studying this line of God dwelling with His people throughout the Old Testament, I gained an appreciation for how long it took and how many challenges had to be surpassed for God to finally dwell with His people in the temple. And even more than that, seeing how distant God used to be from His people, I gained a deep appreciation of our intimate relationship with God today and our ability to be even in the inner chambers with Him.

Understanding this progression of God dwelling with His people I believe is a key to understanding David's heart for God to have a temple. It was a big deal for David to want to build God a house. Not only because the temple would foreshadow God's church, but also because the temple would be the culmination of God's desire of dwelling with His people throughout the centuries leading up to its construction.

Abraham at his Tent

The first man that God called out was Abraham. One of Abraham's encounters with God was in the form of three men coming near his tent. Abraham "ran from his tent door to meet them."[1] He addressed one of the men as "my Lord"[2] and urged them to stay, wash their feet, rest under the tree, and eat some food. Abraham showed them generous hospitality. Although he did not invite them into his tent (in fact there was specific mention that he had to run "from his tent door" in order to meet with them) there was still the thought of giving God a place to stay awhile to be refreshed and satisfied.

Abraham and Sarah prepared a rich meal of cakes, meat, butter, and milk. The thought that might be introduced here is that God wanted to commune with Abraham, and there was the idea of a man providing God with refreshment and satisfaction.

---

1. Gen. 18:2

2. Gen. 18:3

However, there was not yet a thought of God having somewhere to dwell. Abraham needed to plead for the three men to stay—"Do not pass on by Your servant"[3]—because Abraham's place was only a stop for them. What if Abraham had invited them to dwell with him? We can't say for sure what would have happened. Perhaps Abraham would not have dared to ask. But this story shows us the first inklings of God enjoying and getting refreshed by a human being. How wonderful it would have been for Abraham if he had been able to go forward in time and see the tabernacle—a place in the future where there would be no need for God to move on, where food would be constantly provided for Him, and where His presence would be continually among people.

Jacob at Bethel

Two generations later, during Jacob's life, the thought of God dwelling with His people was again mentioned, this time even more directly.[4] Jacob had a dream of a ladder going up to heaven with angels ascending and descending on it. God spoke to him from above the ladder and promised Jacob many descendants—in other words, a household—and promised that He would always be with Jacob—in other words, His presence. Then, when Jacob woke up, he named the place that he had slept "Bethel," which means "house of

---

3. Gen. 18:3

4. Refer to Genesis 28:10–22

13

God."[5] Although there was not yet any form of a physical structure of a house, the house of God seemed to be linked with (1) a place where heaven and earth are connected (by the ladder) and, by extension, where God and mankind are connected; (2) a multi-generational household of people; and (3) a promise of God's presence.

The Israelites in the Wilderness

Mount Sinai

Many years later, when Jacob's descendants had become an entire nation, God had yet more ways to appear to His people before the tabernacle was built. When Jacob's descendants—the children of Israel—were wandering in the wilderness and had come to Mount Sinai, God appeared to them from up the mountain. "Moses brought the people out of the camp to meet with God, and they stood at the foot of the mountain."[6] They had to go *out of the camp* to meet with God because He was not yet dwelling among them in the camp. The people could not even go up the mountain or else they would die. When the Israelites saw the thunder, lightning, and smoke, and heard the trumpets and the voice of God, they became afraid. They took a step back and told Moses to be the mediator between them and God. They said, "If we hear the voice of the LORD our God anymore, then we

---

5. James Strong, *The Exhaustive Concordance of the Bible*.

6. Exod. 19:17

shall die."[7] How serious of a thing it was to be in the presence of God. How deadly it was in the wrong circumstances. How could God ever dwell among His people?

Even worse, when Moses went up the mountain to speak with God, the people made a golden calf and worshiped it. This idolatry angered God and seemed to widen the chasm between Him and His people. It even caused God to want to send His angel before them, rather than go with them Himself. But Moses pleaded, "If Your Presence does not go with us, do not bring us up from here. For how then will it be known that Your people and I have found grace in Your sight, except You go with us?"[8] How much Moses' plea matched what was on God's heart! He also wanted to dwell with His people. He also wanted His very presence to go with them. Moses' plea caused Him to relent and to make a provision for Himself to still be able to go among His "stiff-necked people."[9] At this moment, the desire of a man matched God's desire. It was a mutual desire that God would be among His people. One day, King David would also have a similar prayer, showing that he would also be a man whose desire matched God's desire.

Moses' plea for God to "go with us" eventually led to the plans for the tabernacle, where the presence of God above the ark of testimony could travel with the Israelites. However, before the plans for the tabernacle were laid out, another one of Moses' pleas reminds us

---

7. Deut. 5:25

8. Exod. 33:15–16

9. Exod. 33:3

how serious God's presence was. Moses said, "If now I have found grace in Your sight, O Lord, let my Lord, I pray, go among us, even though we are a stiff-necked people; and pardon our iniquity and our sin and take us as Your inheritance."[10] Moses knew that grace and pardon for iniquity and sin were needed for God to have His presence among His people. Eventually the plans for the tabernacle would include a bronze altar, where animals had to be slaughtered for the people's sins and blood had to be shed in order for the high priest to approach the ark of testimony. Continual shedding of blood was required for God to dwell among His people. This is why, on the mountain, the people could not approach God, and God could not yet come among them.

Moses' Tent

Besides the mountain, there was another way that God spoke with His people. This way came closer to Him dwelling among them, although He was not yet in the camp. Moses took his own personal tent and pitched it outside the camp of the Israelites as a temporary "tabernacle of meeting."[11] The Lord used Moses' house, the house of an individual man who pleased Him, to meet with His people. Yet, He was still not in the camp. He was "outside the camp." In fact, when Moses met with God at his tent, every other Israelite "stood at his tent door" and watched. They watched Moses meet with God from the doors of their

---

10. Exod. 34:9

11. Exod. 33:7

own dwellings. It's interesting that the Bible mentions the doors of their tents, as if to emphasize that the people had to step to the threshold of their dwellings in order to observe God. God was not in their houses; He was observed only after they had come to their tent door. They had their own houses apart from God.

When God spoke to Moses at Moses' tent, a pillar of smoke would descend at the door of Moses' tent. When the people saw this, they "worshiped," but they worshiped "each man in his tent door."[12] Although they were worshiping God, God was still not among them in the way He wanted to be. The people watched and worshiped Him at their doors, then when they were done they went back inside to their houses. God was not a part of their house. He was outside.

This little phrase, "each man in his tent door," stood out to me. Are you like an Israelite who keeps your tent separate from God? Do you have a personal life and then have to step outside your door to be with God or worship Him? Then, after you spend time with Him, do you leave Him outside and retreat back into your personal tent? Do you even watch God work and interact with another person, worshiping Him for what He is able to do in and through that person, but never consider that He wants to come into your space and into your life to the same extent?

Observing God speak to Moses and worshiping Him were very positive things for the Israelites to do, yet we know that the Israelites worshiping at their tent doors was not the full picture of what God wanted. He didn't want to be observed and worshiped from afar, then

---

12. Exod. 33:10

17

left outside as they went back into their personal tents. He wanted to live in their very camp. He ultimately wanted what David would one day also want: "One thing I have desired of the Lord, that will I seek: that I may dwell in the house of the Lord all the days of my life."[13] God wanted eventually to dwell together with mankind, even in the *same house.*

So, by Moses' request and through God's instruction, the tabernacle was established as God's provision for the Israelites to have their God dwelling in their midst. The tabernacle was so connected with His presence: "If Your presence does not go with us, do not bring us up from here." The tabernacle made a way for the presence of God to go with His people from place to place as they followed Him through the wilderness. Here is the heart behind the tabernacle: Lord, we need You; Lord, stay with us. Many of us experience this when we first come to the Lord. We plead for His presence, a genuine confession that we need Him. This is so positive. If Moses didn't ask the Lord on the Israelites' behalf to keep His presence with them, who knows if the tabernacle would have ever been built.

The Tabernacle

Once the tabernacle was built, the sacrifices established, and the priesthood ordained, God dwelt among His people. He dwelt between two cherubim on top of the ark of testimony,[14] a piece of golden furni-

---

13. Ps. 27:4

14. See Exodus 25:10–22

ture placed in the Holy of Holies, a room which only the high priest was allowed to enter once a year, with the shedding of blood. Thus having the presence of God with them in the tabernacle, the Israelites traveled in the wilderness. Each piece of furniture in the tabernacle was built with rings into which poles were slid, so that the Levites could carry the furniture at a moment's notice. Not until they conquered the good land, subdued the other nations, and divided up this new land among the twelve tribes of Israel, did they set up the tabernacle in a more permanent place, in Shiloh.[15] The ark and the tabernacle may have moved around in the good land,[16] but by the time Samuel came on the scene, the tabernacle and ark were in Shiloh and would remain there until an attack from the Philistines.

Samuel in Shiloh

Samuel's mother Hannah consecrated him to serve in the tabernacle, and he began to live there at a very young age.[17] At this time, the people regarded the tabernacle in Shiloh as an established place for them to go and offer to or worship God. Even around the main tent of the tabernacle, "there were buildings erected, which were used partly as a dwelling-place for the officiating priests and Levites, and partly for storing up the heave-offerings, and for preparing the thank-offerings

15. See Joshua 18:1

16. See Joshua 24:25-26 and Judges 20:26–27

17. See 1 Samuel 1:24–28

at the sacrificial meals."[18] Samuel may have lived in these buildings surrounding the tent of meeting, being someone who served so closely with the work in the tabernacle. If what Keil and Delitzsch says is true, that the "whole system of buildings surrounding the tabernacle, with its court and altar of burnt-offering, was called the 'house of God,'"[19] then Samuel, in the only way possible at that time, lived in the house of God. His life foreshadowed the same desire that David would express in many of his Psalms of dwelling in the house of the Lord. Although there would be no solid thought of "dwelling in the house of God" until David's time, here in Shiloh was a sweet picture of young Samuel sleeping in the chambers on the edge of God's house, opening the doors of His house at dawn,[20] and ministering to God inside His house throughout the day. His whole life revolved around the house of God. And although other priests also did the same outwardly, it seems Samuel was the only one who dwelt in the Lord's house in the way that God Himself intended, truly ministering to Him. Samuel was like a shining example of a person living and conducting himself in God's house amid a degraded priesthood. The high priest at the time was Eli, and God exposed the wickedness of Eli's sons, even saying to Eli, "you … honor your sons more than Me."[21] Then God said, "I will raise up for Myself a faithful priest who shall do accord-

---

18. C. F. Keil and F. Delitzsch, *Biblical Commentary on the Old Testament*.

19. Keil and Delitzsch, *Biblical Commentary*.

20. See 1 Samuel 3:15

21. 1 Sam. 2:29

ing to what is in My heart and in My mind. I will build him a sure house, and he shall walk before My anointed forever."[22] God wanted someone who would be faithful to Him, someone who would act in line with what was in God's heart and mind. According to Ellicott, this desire of God was fulfilled by Samuel, who led the nation after Eli's death and worked closely with King Saul, who would become God's anointed king.[23]

Samuel, from his early years to his death, was a picture of a faithful person living and serving in God's house. God even wanted to build Samuel "a sure house," a striking parallel to what God would eventually promise David.

However, the nation of Israel was still far from co-dwelling with God. Samuel was the one positive example, but the sons of Eli, "abhorred the offering of the Lord,"[24] which was the very foundation of mankind being able to step one foot into God's presence, let alone dwell with Him. Additionally, there was not yet any official mention of people dwelling in the house of God. Coates emphasizes this: "In the tabernacle there was no provision for men to dwell in God's house—there was not even a seat there for the priests"[25] as a part of the instructions for building the tabernacle. But when the Bible talks about the temple, "there were 'chambers' (see 1 Kings 6:5, 10), which

---

22. 1 Sam. 2:35

23. C. J. Ellicott, *Commentary for English Readers*.

24. 1 Sam. 2:17

25. Coates, *The House of God*, 52.

suggest the thought of men dwelling in the House of God."[26] King David would be the first to coin the phrase "dwelling in the house of God." He would write about it in many of his Psalms. His interest in dwelling in the house of God would be one of the factors that made him stand out and would perhaps qualify him to be a person who could carry out the transition from the tent to the glorious temple.

The Ark Captured

Then at the end of Eli's life, an unspeakable thing happened to the kingdom of Israel. Several years had passed. Samuel had grown up and seen more and more of the Lord. One day, when Eli had reached the age of ninety-eight, the Israelites went out to Ebenezer to fight against the nation of the Philistines. The Philistines fought back and defeated the Israelites, killing four thousand of their soldiers. This prompted the elders of Israel to ask, "Why has the Lord defeated us today before the Philistines?"[27] But notice that the elders didn't address the Lord directly. We know that Samuel sought direct words from the Lord, for "the LORD revealed Himself to Samuel … by [His] word."[28] However, it seems that the elders did not want God's word. Even though they asked this question, "Why has the Lord defeated us today?" they did not wait to hear His answer. Instead, they

---

26. Coates, *The House of God*, 52.

27. 1 Sam. 4:3

28. 1 Sam. 3:21

got the idea to bring the ark of the covenant out from the tabernacle into the midst of the battle.

After the ark was brought into the battle, the Philistines mustered up all the force they had and fought even harder because they recognized that God was in the camp. They defeated Israel again, scattered them, and killed the high priest's two sons. And then the unimaginable happened: an enemy nation captured the ark of God.

God, "who dwells between the cherubim" on top of the ark,[29] allowed His ark to be stolen by another nation.

What happened here? Why didn't the presence of the ark help the Israelites win the battle, or at least protect them from total defeat? And how could the ark be captured by an enemy nation? Asaph, one of David's singers, would write about this time as a time that God "delivered His strength into captivity, / And His glory into the enemy's hand."[30] How could God allow this to happen? This must have struck the Israelites to the core. In fact, the high priest Eli died on the spot after hearing that the ark was stolen.

In view of the whole Bible, this capture of the ark might not be so strange. We know from Ezekiel 10 that later, when the temple becomes defiled and filled with wickedness, God would have no problem removing His presence from the Holy of Holies there. The dwelling place of a corrupted temple no longer matched Him. So, in this time of Eli and his sons living in wickedness, the capture of the ark was "a practical proof to the degenerate nation, that Jehovah, who was

---

29. 1 Sam. 4:4

30. Ps. 78:61

enthroned above the cherubim, had departed from them."[31] The capture of the ark shows that God was particular about the place He wanted to dwell.

The condition of the Israelites mattered a lot to God. The ark was among God's people but there was something wrong. Although He loved to prove His glory and power to other nations, He would rather allow an apparent failure of His people than affirm a wrong attitude in them.

We are like these Israelites if we "only preach about Him, teach, hear, read, talk, discuss, and dispute about Him, take His name into our mouth, but will not let Him work and show His power in us."[32] Because the Lord has mercy on us, He does not allow these empty efforts to succeed, just as He did not allow His people to succeed on that day of "the greatest calamity"[33] in Israel when God "forsook the tabernacle of Shiloh."[34]

Samuel would go on to show how a nation could rely on God for battle, and we see an example in another battle a few chapters later, a great contrast to the one mentioned above. Before engaging in the battle, Samuel told the Israelites to put away all their idols, he sacrificed a lamb to God, and he cried out to God.[35] Although Samuel did-

---

31. Keil and Delitzsch, *Biblical Commentary*.

32. Berleburger Bible, quoted in Keil and Delitzsch.

33. Ellicott, *Commentary for English Readers*.

34. Ps. 78:60

35. 1 Sam. 7:3, 9

n't have the ark, God answered him and confused the Philistines with thunder so that they were driven out by Israel's forces. Then Samuel set up a stone and called the place Ebenezer, and it is revealed that "this victory was gained in the very same place where the Israelites received their former fatal loss."[36] God didn't tie His presence and His help to that ark. He cared more about the condition of the people, the condition of His *house*.

How important it is for us to be the right people in God's house. The Israelites in Eli's time had the offerings, sacrifices, laws, and requirements for them to be able to be in God's presence. However, because of their lack of obedience to and relationship with God, the presence of God was removed from their midst. How important it is for us, even if we have been redeemed through Christ's sacrifice, to consider our living before God and our relationship with Him, for the sake of His house.

King David

Knowing that God could not be with His people without the shedding of blood *and* that He removed His presence from them when their living didn't match Him, King David's ability not only to restore the ark to Jerusalem but even to make plans for God's house grows more and more incredible. God honored David's desire to build Him a house. This means that David both had the required shedding of blood

---

36. Joseph Benson, *Bible Commentary*.

and was the right person to plan the house of God. In the coming pages and chapters, we will look at David's obstacles, mistakes, actions, and words to see what kind of person he was to be so able in God's eyes to bring about His new, glorious dwelling place.

Shortly after Samuel's death, David began to rule in Judah. The ark, after being captured, had a brief foray in Philistine territory, remained in Abinadab's house for twenty years, was brought by David en route to Jerusalem two separate times, until finally it came to rest in a tent in Jerusalem. The tabernacle had also moved from Shiloh to Gibeon.[37] And the nation of Israel itself had gone through changes, asking God for a king like the other nations, which resulted in the reign of the turbulent and disobedient King Saul. Now that Saul's reign was over and David had become king, Israel could gain more footing as a kingdom, and God could gain more ground in His people.

David as a Picture of the Conquering Christ

David's reign started out with victory. One of David's first acts was to defeat the Jebusites that held the stronghold of Zion,[38] the future location for the City of David, which would be called Jerusalem. After this victory and the gaining of this land, David could then consider the house of God. All of his thoughts for the future temple had to arise from the land being conquered. The temple could not come about if the land was not conquered.

---

37. See 1 Chronicles 21:29

38. See 2 Samuel 5:7

Ever since God's people came to the promised land, they fought to conquer different areas of the land, but they didn't take ownership of the entire land. God had pledged to Abraham that his descendants' land "should reach from a certain river of Egypt to the great Euphrates,"[39] and finally that pledge "was, in fact, realized in David and in his son Solomon."[40] Finally, the fighting was done, and "nothing remained to implement fully God's … pledge except that the Hebrews and their descendants should there abide."[41]

Christ has also come in and secured victory for us in the same way, taking back the "land" from the enemy in such a complete way that nothing remains for us to implement except to abide there. "Christ—the true David—has been made sin in order to put it away by the sacrifice of Himself, … He has annulled death and him who had its power, He has redeemed from the curse those who were under it, He has spoiled principalities and powers, He has put all spiritual enemies under the soles of His feet, … The enemy's power is completely broken."[42] Just as David first secured the entire land before he prepared for the temple, Christ has already conquered sin, death, Satan, and all of their potency, and gained the land on which He is building His church.

---

39. Augustine, *City of God*, trans. Gerald G. Walsh, et al., abridged by Vernon J. Bourke, 380. See Genesis 15:18.

40. Augustine, *City of God*, trans. Walsh et al., 380.

41. Augustine, *City of God*, trans. Walsh et al., 380.

42. Coates, *The House of God*, 47.

Christ *has* conquered. Is this fact infused into our own lives before God? Or do we still doubt who has won? In truth, the outcome is already certain. Christ has conquered everything. Only from the stance that Christ has won the victory can we consider building the house. It is not that we don't need to labor in our Christian lives, but if we are busy fighting battles as if they have not yet been won, with what time will we build up the house? And if we are acting as if the land has not yet been won, then upon what ground can we build anything?

The children of Israel were very good at ignoring the victory that God had won for them. One grievance that would be mentioned about them years later is that, although God delivered them from Egypt, although He led them in the wilderness, although He "cast out from before the children of Israel" the other nations, the Israelites still "walked in the statutes" of the nations that God had conquered for them.[43] They ignored the fact that they had conquered the land, that they were now free from the cultures and laws of the other nations and free to follow their God. They acted as if no victory had been won. Instead, they chose to still follow the statutes of the other nations, as if they were under their rule. They worshiped other nations' gods and walked according to their laws, as if they were enslaved to those nations. How nonsensical this was when we put it like this. But this description was essentially a summary of how "the children of

---

43. 2 Kings 17:8

28

Israel had sinned against the Lord their God"[44] throughout many, many years. Thus, God subjected them to other nations in reality and carried them away in captivity to Assyria and later to Babylon.

How similar we are! Christ has won the victory, yet we often operate as if we are still confined by the laws of the "conquered nations." Then we think that we have to fight a battle all over again with sin, our flesh, and our own desires. This is a difficult reality to be worked out in our lives. Even the Apostle Paul wrote of a conflict he saw in himself, "For I delight in the law of God according to the inward man. But I see another law in my members, warring against the law of my mind, and bringing me into captivity to the law of sin which is in my members."[45] He acknowledges that within the Christian the law of God and the law of sin are at odds. There is a "warring" within him. And it makes us feel like we have to struggle and fight. And it's true; if we stopped there, then we might have to say, "Well, for the rest of our lives we will have to fight against sin and everything else that keeps us from God." But that is not where Paul stops. He goes on in Romans 8 to say that through Jesus Christ, we are *set free* from the "law of sin and death" to be under the new law, the "law of the Spirit of life."[46] We are released from the laws of an enemy nation to be under the laws of the kingdom of our God. We don't have to conquer the law of sin and death; rather, we are already

---

44. 2 Kings 17:7
45. Rom. 7:22–23
46. Rom. 8:2

set free from it, much like the Israelites didn't have to conquer the enemy nations but only had to realize they were free from those nations *and* live in that freedom. Watchman Nee describes these verses from Romans 8 in a very helpful way. He talks about birds. Birds have the "law" of their bird life dictating how they live. They have the life of a bird in them, and that regulates what they can do—they fly. Birds don't have to fight and strive to fly. A law of life is in them that just lets them do that. Now what's a law that counters that flying? The law of gravity. The law of gravity is always there, but the life in the birds overcomes that law. When the life of the bird is gone, or in other words, when the bird dies, then the law of gravity is evident, and the bird falls to the ground. "But while birds live they overcome it," Nee says, "and the life within them is what dominates their consciousness."[47] May the life that is within us dominate our consciousness. May the freedom that we have in Christ dominate our consciousness. And thus may the victory that Christ has won become more real in our day-to-day lives.

David's Desire for God's House

David lived in the good of the victory that God had arranged for him. After he conquered the land, he didn't use the consequent peace and rest to investigate into the customs and religions of the nations around him. He turned his thoughts to serve the God whom he had been set

---

47. Watchman Nee, *The Normal Christian Life*, 196.

free to serve, the God that had conquered the land for him so he could worship unhindered. And he subsequently set his heart on a house he desired to build for God.[48]

Think back for a moment to the initiation of the tabernacle. What had initiated the building of the tabernacle? We saw that Moses had pleaded with God to stay with His people. Moses thought of what the people needed—the presence of their God for security and safety in the face of other nations. The tabernacle was initiated by what God's people needed. How true this is. We need our God.

But David was able to take another step. His life was full of need for the presence of the Lord, and when the Lord was with him and gave him rest, he turned from what *he* needed to what *God* needed. "When many things had gone prosperously with king David, he thought to make a house for God,"[49] revealing "what was most in David's heart. Not the throne…that David should reign. But David's heart thought of Jehovah's throne."[50] Once David had established his kingdom, he turned his mind to what God desired.

This realization seems to be a pivotal moment for many Christians—the realization that it's not only about what *I* want and need, but about what *God* wants and needs. It affects their whole Christian life. It changes the way they view church gatherings: instead of evaluating whether or not the gathering is helpful for them, they think

---

48. See 2 Samuel 7:1–2

49. Augustine, *City of God,* trans. Dods, 512.

50. William Kelly, *William Kelly Commentary.*

about how they can help the church during that gathering. It changes the way they pray: instead of always asking for what they want, they pray to know what is on God's heart and also pray according to His heart as seen in His Word. It changes the way they view people: whether Christians or strangers, they start to consider, "How can I help them grow?" or, "How can I help them know God?" It changes the way they view spiritual food: they are no longer simply the recipient of spiritual food and nourishment, but they realize that, no matter how little they feel they have, they can also feed others.

These two characteristics of David—living in total victory and, as a result of that, considering what was on God's heart—reveal the kind of person he was even before he prepared anything for the temple. He was able to enjoy God's victory to the full, yet without using it to serve himself and his own needs. Instead, David realized that God's victory should result in God's satisfaction, so he used the victory to further God's satisfaction.

From God's point of view, that "gap" between His victory and His satisfaction required the existence of a person who would fully put himself in. God must have been so joyful when David proved to be a person who was after God's heart even when victory came to him. He must have been so joyful when David brought up the matter of a house for God. God waited for David to initiate, just like He waited for Moses' plea on behalf of the people before giving him plans for the tabernacle.

I once spent time with a Christian friend who was frustrated with how little she was growing spiritually. She spent most of her time focusing on her own struggles with and barriers to growing in Christ.

But over the course of several days there was a turning point in her life. She started to care about the growth of others around her. Her heart became filled with how her friends were doing with God. She started asking, "How can I help them grow?" Her fears and frustrations with herself totally dissolved as she touched God's own heart for the people around her.

I believe this is a very real example of learning to live in Christ's victory and turning toward what is on God's heart. My friend didn't solve her issues first. She realized that within her already existed a love and a care for those around her. She could already put herself into what God was doing in people. And she experienced her own struggles and frustrations being taken care of by the Christ who saved her. We have a real victory in Christ that has set us free to chase after what He is after.

We will go on to King David's later life and what it reveals about the character that had developed in him throughout his years of following God, serving God's people, and being shaped by God's interactions with him.

King David's Character

Asaph wrote of David, "he shepherded them according to the integrity of his heart, and guided them by the skillfulness of his hands."[1] What a good pair of attributes. Within, David's heart was full of integrity. Perhaps this meant that he had the right judgment of difficult situations, that he easily had compassion and empathy for the people, or that he loved what was righteous yet lowly and hated what was unrighteous yet praised. The condition of his heart was so important when it came to shepherding God's people. But outwardly, David also had a skill to guide the people. Perhaps this included knowing when to fight and when to retreat, recognizing talents in others to bring them to life, going alongside someone to help them learn a certain craft, or knowing how to gather people and when to gather people and

---

1. Ps. 78:72

which people to gather. David had a heart of integrity *and* skillful hands. Without a heart of integrity, even the most skilled hands would produce what is corrupt, empty, or expedient only for the moment. And without skillful hands, the heart with the most integrity in the world would not know how to bring out its inner intention.

In this section, we will go on to look at both of these attributes of David as it relates to God's house: what was *in his heart* for God's house and how he used *the skill of his hands* for the house, especially leading up to his death and the preparation for the temple. Perhaps we can get a glimpse into Asaph's estimation of David as he interacted face-to-face with his leader and his friend, hearing him speak, watching him carry out his dream for the house of God.

The Census

One event in David's life that revealed the integrity of his heart was actually one of the most shameful moments of the latter part of his reign. Near the end of his life, he numbered the Israelites. The Bible even records that Satan "moved David to number Israel."[2] What a scary thought, to have led God's people for so long yet still be able to be influenced by Satan. Yet, through David's mistake, or rather through his owning of his mistake and his trust in God's mercy for the forgiveness of his mistake, the location for the future building site of

---

2. 1 Chron. 21:1

the temple was determined. We will see how, incredibly, David's repentance in a shameful time led to not only the sin being forgiven but even to the furtherance of the building of the house of God.

Against the council of Joab, David's military leader and companion, David sent out all his leaders to number the people of Israel. As a result of this census, "God was displeased ... [and] struck Israel."[3] David seemed to come to his senses and responded to God, "I have sinned greatly, because I have done this thing; but now, I pray, take away the iniquity of Your servant, for I have done very foolishly."[4] David's ability to own up to his actions was remarkable, considering that he had been serving and leading God's people for years. He had won many victories, yet his heart toward God was as meek and humble as when he was a young shepherd. The attitude in his heart was constant prostration, resonating still with the psalm he wrote earlier— "I acknowledge my transgressions" and "a broken spirit, / A broken and a contrite heart— / These, O God, You will not despise."[5] David cast his blame on no one but himself and looked for deliverance from no one but God. The prophetic couplet, also from his Psalm 51, is so appropriate for a person such as him.

> Then I will teach transgressors Your ways,
> And sinners shall be converted to You.[6]

---

3. 1 Chron. 21:7

4. 1 Chron. 21:8

5. Ps. 51:3, 17

6. Ps. 51:13

As we go on with this story of the census, I pray that we would be taught by David's attitude of repentance and contriteness which prevailed in his life, and may we not rob ourselves of the mercy that David tasted, by thinking that "transgressors" and "sinners" are only those who do not know God. We need to be taught. We need to be converted to God. The Christian who acknowledges his sins or mistakes gets to taste over and over throughout his life the wonderful forgiveness of God, and each time he has a truer, more genuine turning to Him and a truer valuation of His mercy. May we be taught by David's integrity of heart in this respect. May we be impressed by his acknowledgement of his transgressions and his persistent "hope in [God's] mercy."[7]

God had David choose a punishment for his census: either "three years of famine, or three months to be defeated by your foes, ... or else for three days the sword of the Lord—the plague in the land."[8] David's answer was incredible. He said, "I am in great distress. Please let me fall into the hand of the Lord, for His mercies are very great; but do not let me fall into the hand of man."[9] He chose to cast himself back onto the One who was displeased with his action, the One who was exacting the punishment and discipline. This was an incredible

7. Ps. 33:18

8. 1 Chron. 21:12

9. 1 Chron. 21:13

show of his trust in God's mercy. God was the One inflicting him because of his sin. Yet David refused to run away and hide but instead threw himself closer to God. Who could do this? The normal response would be to run away from God, as Adam and Eve did after they transgressed in the garden. Only someone with complete trust in the mercy of God could fling themselves into God's arms when those arms were inflicting a deserved judgment. Somehow, David could admit the wrong yet not turn away from God in shame. He correctly discerned that on the one hand God hated what he had done and there needed to be consequences, but on the other hand God loved David himself, and His mercy for David was endless.

God's mercy for His people resulted in a solution: He told David to build an altar on the threshing floor owned by a certain man, Ornan the Jebusite. (Remember that the Jebusites were the people David and his armies had defeated many years earlier to conquer the stronghold of Zion.) Being king, David could have simply taken the threshing floor from Ornan the Jebusite. After all, Ornan and his people had already been conquered. Ornan even eagerly offers it to David: "Take [the threshing floor] to yourself, and let my lord the king do what is good in his eyes. Look, I also give you the oxen for burnt offerings, the threshing implements for wood, and the wheat for the grain offering; I give it all."[10] But David responds to Ornan, "No, but I will surely buy it for the full price, for I will not take what is yours for the

---

10. 1 Chron. 21:23

39

Lord, nor offer burnt offerings with that which costs me nothing."[11] Then David pays for the location with six hundred shekels of gold.

Why did it happen this way? Hadn't David already conquered all the land? The Jebusites had been defeated, so why couldn't David live in the good of winning the land and just take the threshing floor? The fact that David didn't just take the threshing floor might reveal a principle that is true in our Christian lives. It seems to be a truth that runs parallel to the truth that the land has already been won. On the one hand, we no longer need to fight, but still in our living before God day to day we need to buy. "I will not offer burnt offerings with that which costs me nothing." The threshing floor came at a cost to David.

The security of victory did not lead to passiveness. David saw the need to pay a price in order to build the altar for God. He knew that in order to deliver himself and his people, he could not just offer God what was free and easily available.

A. B. Simpson rightly challenges us: "Beloved, are you giving God that which costs you nothing? Is there real blood in your consecration? Have you ever shed a tear for Christ, or let go a pleasure that some soul might be saved or some cause might be helped for His dear sake?"[12] Like David, our own preparations for the church of God should come at a price. Nothing that is valuable comes cheaply. Have we also, like David, graduated from a cheap life of following

---

11. 1 Chron. 21:24

12. Simpson, *Christ in the Bible*, 355.

God when it suits us or serving Him when it's convenient? When we begin to pay a price, then, and only then, can the building work begin.

So David built the altar on the purchased site "and offered burnt offerings and peace offerings, and called on the Lord."[13] And the Lord withdrew the sword by which He was afflicting the people with plague. It is after this experience that David says "This is the house of the Lord God, and this is the altar of burnt offering for Israel."[14] His experience at Ornan the Jebusite's threshold made him clear that that same location would be the foundation of the temple. How good it was that David bought that threshing floor; otherwise, the entire temple of God would have been on land gifted by another nation, and a conquered nation at that.

This site where the building of the temple would occur represented a lot of things: God's mercy, the redemption of humanity, a servant of God paying a price. It ultimately shows us that the building of the temple is accomplished on the ground of Christ's death, and that we can also enter into that experience of Calvary, where we too sacrifice something of ourselves for the sake of the church.

But at the same time, David could have no boast in having bought the ground for the altar. He was the one in need of the atonement that the altar would provide. Coates describes this threshing floor as "the place of grace and love and sovereign mercy when human failure was

---

13. 1 Chron. 21:26

14. 1 Chron. 22:1

complete and on man's side everything was forfeited."[15] We see in David a complete surrender and repentance toward God, and a deep love and trust toward Him that went all the way to the end of his strength, all the way to the bottom of his failure.

There is a verse in a hymn by Anna Waring that seems to describe David in this moment:

> On Thee my humbled soul would wait,
> Her utmost weakness calmly learning.
> And see Thy grace its way create
> Through thorns and briers which Thou art burning.[16]

David exhibited this attitude his whole life. When the Lord showed through His light some thorns and briers in his heart or a misled path in his life, he had genuine repentance. He quietly and "calmly" allowed God to show him his "utmost weakness." Then he acknowledged and accepted God's estimation of him without excuse or rebuttal. Only then could the "way" be made through the "thorns and briers." Only then could he go on, through God's grace alone, to build something with Him. God's grace created a way for the temple to come in. But in order for that to happen, David needed to be a man with humbled soul, calmly waiting on God, learning his utmost weakness, and allowing God to burn through the thorns and briers in him. Then, God could make a way for the temple.

---

15. Coates, *The House of God*, 51.

16. From "Source of My Spirit's Deep Desire."

Blocked from Building the Temple

Years later, Solomon would in fact build the temple at this same threshing floor.[17] It was through David's acknowledgement of his sin, his repentance, and his clinging to God that the location was determined. And it was through his desire to pay a price for God that the location was bought.

But there was yet a greater example of David's surrender and repentance toward God: his response to God when God told him he could not build the temple. In 1 Chronicles 22:8, God spoke to David and said, "You have shed much blood and have made great wars; you shall not build a house for My name, because you have shed much blood on the earth in My sight." And then instead of David, God designated David's son Solomon to build His house.

David could have responded to God in so many ways. He could have argued, "But God, didn't I shed that blood for You? Didn't I secure Zion and bring about peace for the Israelites through that shed blood?" Or he could have argued, "Wasn't building the house my idea? Without me, You wouldn't even have a house. What do you mean You will build the house without me?" He also could have gotten bitter and said, "Fine, if You don't want me to build it, that's the end of that matter for me. I will focus on other things if that's what You want." He could also have gotten upset with himself, become mopey, and wallowed around condemning himself for not being able

17. See 2 Chronicles 3:1

43

to build the temple. Either way, whether he cast the temple out of his mind out of bitterness, or despaired of his shortcomings and mistakes, he would not have done anything for God's house. But, as we saw before with David keeping himself close to the Lord's hands and accepting His judgment, He took what God said, the limitation He gave, and still gave everything he could possibly give, up to that limitation. This again reveals the integrity that was in his heart. It was as if David said, "I hear what God has said. But I will still do everything within the bounds that He set. If I can't build the house, I will do everything that is physically possible for the house except build it."

Imagine if preaching before a congregation was the one way that you dreamed of serving Him, and you even had a conviction that preaching was a way God really wanted to use to reach people. And then imagine that one day He told you, "You cannot preach. I will use someone else for this." Would you throw in the towel and say, "I'm done serving You, You are too unfair." Or would you instead put your whole being into supporting that other one through whom the Lord would speak. Would you still put yourself in by inviting people to the preaching, cooking a meal for people to enjoy after the preaching, or in prayer laboring that the preaching would really bless God? A. B. Simpson says that at the end of his life, David "labored as unselfishly for the temple that Solomon should build as if he himself had been entrusted with the entire task." And then he asks us, "have we learned to take as much delight in God's work through the hand of another as when it bears the impress of our own personality? ... No man is ready to say, 'Here am I. Send me' until he has first learned to say, 'Lord, send who you want to send.'"[18]

David's reaction to God's limitation on him reveals a deep acceptance of God's judgment, even deeper than his response after the census. After the census, David acknowledged his sin, turned back to God, and accepted the consequences without excuse. However, here, it was a characteristic of David's life that made him unfit to build the temple. When there is sin involved, it would be difficult to respond as David responded. How often have we sinned against someone, including God, and held back some feeling because we believed we somehow had an excuse or a good reason for behaving the way we did? David was not this way even when God pointed out something in his life that actually forwarded God's purpose. David's care for God and His house overrode any rebuttal or vindication or bitterness that might have consumed him. David could have easily said, "Didn't the blood I shed secure this kingdom?" But instead David acknowledged the judgment placed upon him, soberly accepted God's estimation of him, and was content with the place God put him in, simply because that was what God decided.

David had learned to accept the truth that Paul would eventually write about in Romans 9: "It is not of him who wills, nor of him who runs, but of God who shows mercy."[19] His utmost trust in God and his utmost honor for the will of God made him a man able to accept any word out of God's mouth. But he did not become this way overnight. After he committed adultery with Bathsheba and ordered the murder

---

18. Simpson, *Christ in the Bible*, 362 (note from previous page).

19. Rom. 9:16

of Uriah, his only plea was the mercy of the Lord. When Shimei was cursing him during his exile, he did nothing to stand up for himself but rather said, "let him curse, because the Lord has said to him, 'Curse David.' Who then shall say, 'Why have you done so?'"[20] In the seventh psalm, he laid himself and his actions completely open to God and wrote:

> If there is iniquity in my hands,
> If I have repaid evil to him who was at peace with me,
> Or have plundered my enemy without cause,
> Let the enemy pursue and overtake me;
> Yes, let him trample my life to the earth,
> And lay my honor in the dust.[21]

David had no false sense of righteousness. He knew what kind of person he was and what he was capable of. Even when cursed by a man, seemingly wrongly, he took it for God's words. He regarded his fallen state as a man in a sober way, giving way neither to false pride nor self-absorbed despair.

All his life, David hoped in God's mercy. Every step he took, every mistake he made, he threw himself back upon the Lord because of his hope in His mercy. He was not afraid to be weak and vulnerable before God, as he trusted in Him to the utmost, so much so that he chose continually to expose himself before Him at the lowest times in

---

20. 2 Sam. 16:10

21. Ps. 7:3–5

his life. His integrity of heart was not innate human virtues that he could boast of and lean on when times got tough. His integrity of heart had everything to do with a sober judgment of himself and the ability to cast himself before God, even in his darkest moments.

Ability to Translate a Pattern into Something Greater

Having no self-righteousness and no boast in himself did not make David a floundering helpless noodle of a king. David had a lot of skill and put it to use for God. His humility before God did not paralyze him. It did not make him unable to do anything worthwhile. Rather, because he was so truly humble and empty before God, it enabled him to be greatly used and filled up with the things of God.

There is a great example of this when David was drawing up plans for the temple. Have you ever considered why he didn't just make another tabernacle? The tabernacle had been so significant in its symbols and details. Every step had been outlined by the Spirit of God and was full of meaning. Hebrews 9:8–9 even talks about the Holy Spirit arranging the details in the tabernacle because today they indicate spiritual principles for the lives of Christians. And when we look at how the tabernacle was made, the craftsman Bezalel was filled "with the Spirit of God in wisdom, in understanding, in knowledge, and in all manner of workmanship, to design artistic works…"[22] Down to the very colors of the linens, every detail of the tabernacle

22. Exod. 31:3–4

was inspired by the Spirit of God. It would have made sense for David to go with what the Spirit said before in order to preserve the symbolism of all that the tabernacle represented.

However, when David set out to build another house for God, he didn't just copy the original tabernacle. He was able to take the core ideas of the tabernacle and translate them into something greater. On one hand, he didn't go rogue and make whatever he could come up with on his own, but on the other hand he also didn't just remake the tabernacle.

Why was this? Perhaps he understood that the tabernacle itself was made "according to the pattern which was shown [Moses] on the mountain."[23] Moses received a pattern to create the tabernacle from God Himself. In any case, David knew he had to be in tune with a new, current speaking of the Spirit of God.

In 1 Chronicles 28, David gathered the leaders of Israel to hand the kingdom over to his son. A portion of the chapter is printed below. As you read it, pay attention to each detail of the temple.

> Then David gave his son Solomon the plans for the vestibule, its houses, its treasuries, its upper chambers, its inner chambers, and the place of the mercy seat; and the plans for all that he had by the Spirit, of the courts of the house of the Lord, of all the chambers all around, of the treasuries of the house of God, and of the treasuries for the dedicated things; also for the division of the priests and the Levites, for all the work of the service of the house

---

23. Exod. 25:40

of the Lord, and for all the articles of service in the house of the Lord. He gave gold by weight for things of gold, for all articles used in every kind of service; also silver for all articles of silver by weight, for all articles used in every kind of service; the weight for the lampstands of gold, and their lamps of gold, by weight for each lampstand and its lamps; for the lampstands of silver by weight, for the lampstand and its lamps, according to the use of each lampstand. And by weight he gave gold for the tables of the showbread, for each table, and silver for the tables of silver; also pure gold for the forks, the basins, the pitchers of pure gold, and the golden bowls—he gave gold by weight for every bowl; and for the silver bowls, silver by weight for every bowl; and refined gold by weight for the altar of incense, and for the construction of the chariot, that is, the gold cherubim that spread their wings and overshadowed the ark of the covenant of the Lord. "All this," said David, "the Lord made me understand in writing, by His hand upon me, all the works of these plans."[24]

The plans that David gave to Solomon for the temple were so detailed that he even knew the weight of gold required to make the forks. "All of this" he knew because "the Lord made [him] understand in writing, by His hand upon [him], all the works of these plans." These were not plans that David arbitrarily came up with according to how he understood the big picture. No, even these minute plans were given to him "by the Spirit."

---

24. 1 Chron. 28:11–19

What do these verses indicate to us? First, it shows us that the Spirit is full of details. Imagine how many more details would have had to be in the full blueprint for the temple! How many separate blueprints there must have been for each floor, for the gates in the walls, the courts, the chambers, and all the pieces of furniture! The Spirit revealed to David the works of all those plans. He didn't just inspire the big dream for the temple. The Spirit actually issued out an abundance of details for the temple.

I'll say that again. The Spirit doesn't just inspire big dreams. The spirit issues out such an abundance of details, we can't even imagine it. Perhaps the Spirit has a thought, and we can usually latch on to that thought, but we should also know that all the details that fill out the thought are in the Spirit's mind too. And the details of the details. And the details of the details of the details. Imagine being in space with the Spirit of God and looking at planet Earth. The Spirit tells you, "This is Earth, My creation." You look at it and admire the blue seas, the green land, the white clouds. Then the Spirit says, "Come closer." So you draw nearer to the earth, through the atmosphere to the level of the clouds. Wow, now you can see that the earth is made up of different biomes. Savannahs, rainforests, mountains, and each one so unique and beautiful. The Spirit says again, "Come closer." And you get closer to the biomes and see that there are communities and cities in those biomes, and then the Spirit ushers you in further and you realize the cities are made up of crowds, and the crowds are made up of individual people, and then you get close to one person and you realize they have different organs, and the organs have different types of tissues, and the tissues are made up of different cells, and even the cells have their own organelles, all the way down to the tiniest ribosome. And you got all of that starting from one broad view of planet Earth. How much do we miss because we remain out in space only admiring the blue seas and green land!

What does this mean for our own life of serving God? As an example, let's say that you have a feeling to hold an event for high schoolers. You even have a burden for the event: to help the high schoolers start to love the Bible. How can we approach planning this event in the same way that David approached planning the temple? Just by asking ourselves questions about the event, we can see how many details are necessary in planning. How long should it be? Where should it be held? Who should help serve? Should we have formal gatherings or just hanging out? Should it be one longer event or should it be several shorter events carried out over a month's time? What should we talk about? Should we eat together? Should we sing? What songs should we sing? Should we read the Bible? What should we read?

So often we can either assume the answers to these questions because of what we are used to or how we think something should be carried out. We may think, "Of course we would read the Bible. We want them to learn to love the Bible. Let's read verses about the value of reading the Bible." It might seem obvious. But does that match the Spirit's answer to those same questions? We can't know until we ask Him.

How would our serving be different if we realized that the Spirit has an answer to every one of these questions? These details are not beyond Him. No question is too insignificant for Him. In fact, He would love for us to come to Him asking for as much detail as David received for the temple.

From God's interaction with David, we see that He cares that we *understand* His plans. David says "the Lord made me *understand* in writing." Do we realize that the Spirit is this practical? We often think the Spirit gives us feelings or impressions. We expect that when we're filled with the Spirit we will have a sense of God or a sense of power. But have you considered that when you're filled with the Holy Spirit, you know blueprints for a building? We also could be filled with the Holy Spirit to know what the high school event should look like, how many gatherings to have, when to sing and when to just talk, even down to what Bible passage to read. Through the Spirit, we, like David, can know not only what to feel in our hearts, but what to do with our hands.

How do we actually get to know God's thoughts about each detail? Is it something He will just tell us? David's experience was: "the Lord made me understand in writing, *by His hand upon me*, all the works of these plans." It took time for David to understand the plans, and it took God's hand upon him. David had to *allow* the Lord's hand to rest upon him. Think of the temple blueprints—all the measurements, the angles, the materials—everything would need to be learned. It took God's "hand upon [David]" to come into an understanding of all those plans. How much time David must have spent under God's hand! He had much reason to hustle and bustle about, gathering supplies, communicating with people. But he also must have had still, quiet moments in his heart, coming before God and waiting for God to rest His hand on him.

When the Spirit does give us a broad feeling or a sense, it takes time in prayer, remaining with Him, to let that broad sense get broken down into its component parts. Imagine being in space again. Often our interaction with the Spirit goes like this: we see the earth, we see the biomes, we see the cities, and then we say, "that's good enough, I can fill the rest in." But the Spirit wants to *show* us the crowds, the people, the organs, down to the very molecules that are passing in and out of the cells. If we stay under the Lord's hand rather than coming out from under it, we would see just how detailed the Spirit is. The Spirit's thought would be opened up to us like a beautiful kaleidoscope, the colorful fractals happily revealed before our eyes, and we would be in amazement. Then we would be fit to carry out with our hands what the Spirit has made us understand in our hearts.

King David was a person able to know the Spirit in a present, detailed way, able to let the Spirit give him understanding and show him an abundance of details as well as the big picture. Because of this, he had a way to translate what the Spirit revealed in the past into the current, relevant situation. He let the Spirit inform the actions of his hands. May we all develop this creativity, flexibility, and sensitivity to act and plan according to what the Spirit is doing.

King David's Motivations

We've seen the type of person David was, as evidenced by his response to God at different junctures in his life. He was repentant when God exposed his sin, he was accepting when God limited his work, and he was attentive when God desired to show him plans for His temple. But what motivated David to throw everything he had into the preparation for God's house? Of course, he had a deep love for God Himself, but what else do David's words and actions reveal as the driving force behind all of his preparations?

An Affection for God and His work

As David handed the kingdom off to Solomon before the assembly of Israel, he said before all the people, "because I have set my affection on the house of my God, I have given to the house of my God, over and above all that I have prepared for the holy house, my own special treasure of gold and silver."[1] The house of God wasn't just a project for David. It wasn't just a task to fulfill. His affection was directed toward it. This phrase in the NKJV translation is very interesting. David "set" his affection on the house. When there were a lot of other things that David could have *set* his affection on—his kingship, his power, his material possessions—he chose to set his affection on God's house.

At what point was his affection set for God's house? C. A. Coates thinks that David had thoughts for God's house far earlier than his prayer in 2 Samuel 7.

> From the very beginning of David's history he had the House of God before him. I think we may gather this from Psalm 132. In the time of David's afflictions he devoted himself to "find out a place for the Lord, an habitation for the mighty God of Jacob"; and he says in verse 6, "Lo, we heard of it at Ephratah; we found it in the fields of the wood." When he was living in Bethlehem and wandering in the fields—long before he came to the kingdom—the house of God was before him, and he came to the kingdom really to prepare for the building of the house.[2]

---

1. 1 Chron. 29:3

2. Coates, *The House of God*, 48.

56

If this is true, then it wasn't when David had come into power that he suddenly turned his thoughts to God's house. His thoughts of God's house were nurtured and treasured up throughout his earlier life. He didn't need a position to start to care about God's house. If he thought that once he became king *then* he would focus on God because of his position and duty, then when he finally became king he might have been swept away with anything and everything else involved in being a king. He didn't start to care about God's house because he became king. He was a person who cared about God's house, and when he became king, he was able to act on the desires of his heart.

May we also not reserve our feelings and thoughts for God for a time when we are called into some service. Like David, let us not think that, when we are given some role or position, *then* we will turn our hearts and attention to God. If we can become people who care about God in our busy work lives or school lives or family lives, then when we do have a chance to serve or fill a certain role, our work for God won't come out of that role we've been given, but out of a desire for God's house that we have cultivated and allowed to grow throughout many years. The role we are given may be as short-term as taking care of the children during one church service. Or it may be a calling to quit your job and enter full-time ministry. Either way, God is not looking for good role-fillers who can care for God's house. He is looking for *people* who care about God's house, even during a busy semester schedule or a stressful work week. May *who we are* dictate our serving life before God rather than the position we occupy.

David definitely didn't care for God's house only on the basis of being a king. He did give the treasures he won as a king to the house.[3] But, there was also a portion of the materials that did not come from David's work and responsibility as king. There was a portion of materials that came from his life as a human being before God. "Because I have set my affection on the house of my God, I have given to the house of my God, over and above all that I have prepared for the holy house, *my own special treasure* of gold and silver."[4]

It seems like, when David spoke this sentence, he stepped out of his position as king. I picture him removing his crown before all the leaders of Israel, stepping off the platform from which he had previously addressed them, and saying, "I have told you what I have gathered as a king. Now I will tell you what I have given as a man who is in love with God. I gave my own special treasure. I wasn't content with just satisfying my duty and service. I gave from my own treasure, my own livelihood, my own most precious things." In this moment, it feels like we are seeing David once again as the shepherd boy who entrusted his flock and his own life to his God. He didn't one day step into the position of king and then become wholly for God. No, he loved and treasured God all his life, and the proportion of his life which he had offered to God as a shepherd was the same as the proportion he now offered as a king. He didn't have personal gold and

---

3. C. A. Coates notes the symbolism of the conquered or gifted treasure from other nations: "It suggests to me that all the fruit and spoil of Christ's victory, and all that has accrued to Him as the exalted One, goes to enrich and beautify the House of God" (*The House of God*, 51).

4. 1 Chron. 29:3 (emphasis mine)

silver as a shepherd, but what he did have he fully entrusted to God. And even though he now had access to so much wealth and resources, he wasn't content until he had given from his own personal treasure. It wouldn't have mattered if during his reign he had conquered three times the nations and plundered three times the treasure. He would still have desired, as a man, to give something from his "own special treasure." This truly speaks to a great affection toward God and His house.

I also like the NASB translation of this same verse: "in my delight in the house of my God, the treasure I have of gold and silver, I give to the house of my God, over and above all that I have already provided for the holy temple." We see that David's positive feeling for God's house results in an action. As a result of his delight in it, he gave to the house of his God his own special treasure of gold and silver.

What if we, like David, just couldn't be content with our spiritual service until it elicited from us, not only what it is our duty to give, but what we personally treasure. I'm reminded of the widow in Mark 12. Other richer people gave their tithes, offering what it was their duty to offer. But the widow offered "her whole livelihood."[5] Her offering came from what little she had for herself. It came from how she was going to get dinner that night. It came from her whole life and being.

---

5. Mark 12:44

Imagine a person who has been tasked with preparing drinks for a church event. Let's say that this person has been considering this event a lot. They realize that God could change lives at this event, and they hope that He does. Then, they consider how their drink service can support God getting what He is after. They may say, "I want people to feel loved here. I want someone who is here for their first time to feel cared for." Then, perhaps they use a lunch break at work to find recipes for good drinks, or they stay up an hour later at night to research how to make the perfect batch of percolated coffee. They go above and beyond their duty because of an affection for the house of God that already exists in them. And they give out of their own personal time to help the house of God, not just what it is their duty to give for the event.

May we flee from a life that is simply doing our duty. May we have a life where our affection for God's house causes us to give out of our personal time, our personal energy, our personal life. If offering like this seems too hard or too far from us, we can pray, "Lord, increase my affection for Your house." It was David's affection that caused him to give from his own reserves, and it is our affection that will draw out into our willing, extended hands, what we had previously kept back for ourselves as most precious, even all that we had to live on.

After telling the crowd of Israelites about his gift to God from his own special treasure, David then asked a question that struck a chord in everyone's heart: "Who then is willing to consecrate himself to the Lord?"[6] After seeing and hearing David's affection and his example, who could not but respond to this call? The leaders of Israel willingly "gave for the work of the house of God five thousand talents and ten thousand darics of gold, ten thousand talents of silver, eighteen thousand talents of bronze, and one hundred thousand talents of iron. And whoever had precious stones gave them to the treasury of the house of the Lord."[7] And then what did the people do after they offered to God? They "rejoiced, for they had offered willingly."[8] What a glorious experience!—God working in the people through David's example to willingly give to Him, and this very action issuing out abundant joy! We could be as contagious as David, through our own example also causing others to joyfully give their time and precious things. Instead of compelling others to serve God, could there be in our being, characterized by our affection for God and our offering out of our own treasure, something that sparks the same response in other people?

The nation, made willing and eager by David's example, could now respond to David's previous charge: "Now set your heart and your soul to seek the Lord your God. Therefore arise and build the sanctuary of the Lord God, to bring the ark of the covenant of the Lord and the holy articles of God into the house that is to be built for the name of the Lord."[9]

---

6. 1 Chron. 29:5 (note from previous page)

7. 1 Chron. 29:7–8

8. 1 Chron. 29:9

9. 1 Chron. 22:19

61

A Care for Solomon and the Coming Generations

David's willingness to gather materials for the temple was also evidence of a care for people beyond his lifetime. He invested himself in what he would never be able to see. He sowed seeds that he would never be able to reap. His vision was not confined to his own life and times. How different he was from King Hezekiah! King Hezekiah revealed where his cares lay when Isaiah prophesied to him that God would delay the captivity of Israel until after Hezekiah had passed away. Immediately Hezekiah responded, "The word of the Lord which you have spoken is good! ... Will there not be peace and truth at least in my days?"[10] What small-mindedness! Because of his narrow view, Hezekiah did nothing to stop the eventual downfall of his country. He cared only for the prosperity of his own life.

David, on the other hand, although he knew he would not live to see the fruit of his labor, put his hands to work to bless the future generations of God's kingdom. His peace and hope were not only connected to the kingdom's prosperity in his life, but it was tied to his assurance that his descendants would prosper. This is why David could write such things like, "My flesh also will rest in hope. / For You will not ... / ... allow Your Holy One to see corruption."[11] He had an assurance that *after* his life, his seed would thrive, and that was a cause of rest and peace for him *during* his life. He knew "that God

10. 2 Kings 20:19

11. Ps. 16:9–10

had sworn with an oath to him that of the fruit of his body, according to the flesh, He would raise up the Christ to sit on his throne."[12] And this Christ would be referred to as the son of David. What an honor for the Messiah to be connected to David in this way, skipping all the generations between. And yet how fitting too because of the care David had and the peace it brought him to know that, through his seed, the kingdom of God would be secure. Romans 1:3 gives a shout-out to David, harkening back to David's assurance for his seed and acknowledging Jesus as "born of the seed of David according to the flesh." And how gladly God Himself must have said of David, "My mercy I will keep for him forever, / ... his seed also I will make to endure forever, / And his throne as the days of heaven."[13] These promises to David were fulfilled. Not only did David "never lack a man to sit on the throne of the house of Israel,"[14] but Jesus became the ultimate fulfillment of that promise, the "Branch of righteousness,"[15] growing up out of David's seed, the One who truly would endure forever and whose throne would truly be as the days of heaven.

David's care for the coming generations caused him to take specific and actionable steps. We could have a general feeling that the young generation is the future, or a general hope that those after us would

---

12. Acts 2:30

13. Ps. 89:28–29

14. Jer. 33:17

15. Jer. 33:15

rise up and bless the church, but we can also, like King David, put ourselves in to be a part of bringing our hopes to fruition. Our own actionable steps might include something as small as transcribing the speaking of a minister in order to preserve it, not because there is any current request for it to be read, but because in 200 years someone might find it and benefit from it. Or we might do something as immediate as shepherding a younger Christian who has a real desire for God, with the realization that they may in their later life go on to bless thousands of people. One of Moses' sons, Eliezer, had an only son, Rehabiah. The Bible records specifically that "Eliezer had no other sons, but the sons of Rehabiah were very many."[16] And then later, Rehabiah and his sons are listed after Eliezer.[17] Although after one generation Eliezer had only one descendant, time showed just how fruitful he would become through that one. Let's not look down on who we can immediately influence or cause to grow. They may go on to serve and affect millions.

This heart of David, the heart that many people after him would thrive in God's kingdom, was also the heart of God the Father, who desired that through the Son of David, even more sons would be gained. Jesus would become the grain of wheat that fell to the ground, giving rise to many grains. God had this in His mind even in David's day, and David somehow stepped into that same thought, that God wanted many more to come into His household, both immediately following David's lifetime and many centuries later, even up to today. May we also step into that realization that God wants to usher people into His house for generations to come.

A Desire to Live in God's House

Perhaps David had such a care for the future generations coming into God's house because he himself deeply longed to live in God's house. One of the dearest and sweetest aspects of David's life before the Lord was his love of dwelling with his God. I mentioned previously that before David, there was no talk of dwelling in God's house. "During the time the tabernacle was still being moved from place to place we hear no such mention of dwelling in God's tabernacle or house. It was David who coined this expression for loving fellowship with the God of revelation, simultaneously with his preparation of a settled dwelling-place for the sacred Ark."[18]

We see this thought of dwelling in God's house in many of David's Psalms:

> Blessed is the man You choose,
> And cause to approach You,
> That he may dwell in Your courts.
> We shall be satisfied with the goodness of Your house,
> Of Your holy temple.[19]

---

16. 1 Chron. 23:17 (note from previous page)

17. See 1 Chronicles 26:25 (note from previous page)

18. Keil and Delitzsch, *Biblical Commentary*.

19. Ps. 65:4

For You have been a shelter for me,
A strong tower from the enemy.
I will abide in Your tabernacle forever;
I will trust in the shadow of Your wings.[20]

How precious is Your lovingkindness, O God!
Therefore the children of men put their trust under the shadow of
Your wings.
They are abundantly satisfied with the fullness of Your house,
And You give them drink from the river of Your pleasures.[21]

One thing I have desired of the Lord,
That I will seek:
That I may dwell in the house of the Lord
All the days of my life,
To behold the beauty of the Lord,
And to inquire in His temple.
For in the time of trouble
He shall hide me in His pavilion;
In the secret place of His tabernacle
He shall hide me.[22]

---

20. Ps. 61:3–4

21. Ps. 36:7–8

22. Ps. 27:4–5a

> Surely goodness and mercy shall follow me
> All the days of my life;
> And I will dwell in the house of the Lord
> Forever.[23]

> Lord, who may abide in Your tabernacle?
> Who may dwell in Your holy hill?
> He who walks uprightly,
> And works righteousness,
> And speaks the truth in his heart.[24]

We could dig into each of these passages in themselves. But a broad stroke shows David's thoughts of abiding in God's house forever, being satisfied with God's house, being protected or hidden in God's house, and conducting himself in God's house. Coates puts it well: "We get [in the thought of dwelling in God's house] the consciousness that His place is our place. We have not only a way of approach, but a home."[25] David took the idea of God dwelling among His people to a whole new level. God's house was not to be only a place for

---

23. Ps. 23:6

24. Ps. 15:1–2

25. Coates, *The House of God*, 55.

worship. God's house was to be a place where His people could also live. It was no longer everyone living in their own dwellings surrounding God's dwelling. David introduced the thought that people and God would live in the *same dwelling*.

Another idea that David introduced was the playing of music in God's house for the people to enjoy and use in worship to God. "While there was no song in connection with the tabernacle," with the temple "they had reached the favored hour when their toil was over, and they could happily and restfully raise their song in the House of the Lord."[26] There are numerous psalms by David that mention making music to the Lord. The psalms themselves were put to music. And David designated certain families of the Levites to "prophesy with harps, stringed instruments, and cymbals."[27]

In this singing and music-making we see a metaphor for us today, that "it is possible to retire from the wilderness, and even from the bearing of burdens in service and testimony here, and to reach a spot in spirit where we can sing as those who participate in the fatness, blessedness, and joy of God's house."[28] The people no longer needed to wander the wilderness tired and dirty; they no longer needed to strive to fight off their enemies; there was now room for celebration and enjoyment in the land.

---

26. Coates, *The House of God*, 56.

27. 1 Chron. 25:1

28. Coates, 56.

David had unlocked these two truths about God's house: God's house was a home not only for God, but for His people, and it was a place not only to serve and bear the burdens of the house, but to sing and rejoice. And because David longed to experience these delights of God's house himself, and because he cared for generations after him, he put in everything he possibly could to ensure that those after him would get to enjoy something he had dreamed about his whole life but would never see.

With these three motivations—a true affection for God and His house, a care for the coming generations, and a desire to live in God's house—David had the energy to spur on the preparation for a marvelous temple that would bring about God's glory on the earth.

The Temple

An impressive structure was constructed on the earth in the days of Solomon. Two giant pillars stood at its entrance, decorated with garlands of pomegranates.[1] A huge bronze basin sat in the middle of the court, resting on the backs of twelve bronze statues of oxen.[2] Through golden doors was the vestibule, filled with golden walls carved with palm trees and cherubim.[3] Ten golden lampstands and ten golden tables sat along those walls. Every utensil for maintaining the lampstands and tables were made of gold.[4] From the small golden utensils to the great size of the temple itself, everything boasted of the wealth of the kingdom.

---

1. 2 Chron. 3:15–17
2. 2 Chron. 4:2–4, 10
3. 2 Chron. 3:5–7
4. 2 Chron. 4:7–8, 22

Through Solomon's "well-ordered" work,[5] the temple was finished and the ark of the covenant was brought in to be, at last, reunited with the house of God. The priests, singers, and people of Israel sang with cymbals, harps, and trumpets, and as they were singing and praising God with one voice, "the glory of the Lord filled the house of God."[6]

This magnificent picture, the pinnacle of God dwelling with His people on the earth in the Old Testament, holds a lot of significance for us. In the same way that the glory filled the physical temple, the glory and presence of God will one day fill His church in a fully magnified way.

Two metaphors stand out when considering this age of the temple, and those are (1) the Father's house and (2) Christ as a conquering King.

The Father's House

Remember the voice booming on the mountain back in Exodus, the distance between God and His people because of sin, and the fear of the people to come even close to being close to God? How drastic the difference is with this scene at the dedication of the temple, where the people are able to stand before God's presence and sing praise to

---

5. 2 Chron. 8:16

6. 2 Chron 5:14

Him. Rather than trembling, the people are joyful. Rather than telling Moses to intercede for them, the people are uttering praise to God out of their own lips. Rather than shying away from the terrifying presence of God, the people even bring in His presence.

One main difference between the mountain and the temple was that with the temple (as with the tabernacle) there was a shedding of blood on behalf of the people. There were many sacrifices carried out by the priests that brought the people closer to God. Built into the very temple structure was a way for forgiveness of sins, for peace with God, for fellowship with God, and many other blessings that connected the people to their God in a way that they could not obtain themselves.

Today, Jesus has come to be the sacrifice "once for all."[7] Our relationship with God today is not like those Israelites at the base of the mountain, but it is instead like the Israelites at the dedication of the temple where, at last, God was able to get what He desired—a dwelling place with His people in perfect peace and intimacy.

When I look back from the beginning of God's journey with His people, I can't help but think of His heart as a Father. At the beginning, there was no way for Him to be with His people. But after implementing a way for His people to come to Him through blood, He could finally dwell among them as fully as He could at the time. And now, after sending His beloved Son as a sacrifice for us, the Father is

---

7. Heb. 9:12

finally able to get what He desires: a people who can joyfully and without an ounce of unease enter into His house, not only as honored guests but as beloved children coming home.

> For you have not come to the mountain that may be touched and that burned with fire, and to blackness and darkness and tempest, and the sound of a trumpet and the voice of words, so that those who heard it begged that the word should not be spoken to them anymore....
>
> But you have come to Mount Zion and to the city of the living God, the heavenly Jerusalem, to an innumerable company of angels, to the general assembly and church of the firstborn ... to Jesus the Mediator of the new covenant, and to the blood of sprinkling that speaks better things than that of Abel.[8]

Jesus Himself began to usher people into His Father's house while He was on earth. "In My Father's house are many mansions; if it were not so, I would have told you. I go to prepare a place for you."[9] How did Jesus prepare a place for us? He said this before being crucified, ris-

---

8. Heb. 12:18–19, 22–23a, 24

9. John 14:2

ing from the dead, and ascending to the Father in heaven. Because of His sacrifice, we know that we are coming to the Father's house—not a physical house and "not made with hands,"[10] but a spiritual one that we can experience and love today despite not yet having it in full.

For truly, our entrance into the Father's house isn't only reserved for that day in which we will fully and perfectly dwell with Him. Even today, "in spirit it is our privilege to taste the holy joy of being brought by the Son into the chambers of the Father's house."[11] Do we not experience God's house today, in the love of fellow Christians, in the acceptance that we feel knowing that we are forgiven, in the leading deep inside our hearts drawing us to come closer, always closer to the God of our salvation? How marvelous and heartfelt it is that God allows us to feel, even before we know it in reality, "the Son [leading us] into the chambers of the Father's house." How intimate, how secure. My heart is filled with thankfulness after studying this broad sweep of God's house, all the way from the scary voice on the mountain distanced by fear, to the Father drawing us into His very chambers to be with us and to talk to us. We are brought so near after being so far away. We are like poor homeless criminals being brought into the chambers of a king. Each of us could testify that God has truly brought "a poor vile sinner into his 'house of wine!'"[12]

---

10. Heb. 9:11

11. Coates, *The House of God*, 55.

12. From "O Christ He Is the Fountain" by Anne R. Cousin.

Solomon as a Picture of the Reigning Christ

Psalm 72 says of Solomon that "He will judge [God's] people with righteousness, / And [His] poor with justice. / ... He will bring justice to the poor of the people; / He will save the children of the needy, / And will break in pieces the oppressor. / ... In His days the righteous shall flourish, and abundance of peace...."[13] This psalm is in part speaking of the man Solomon and also truly prophesying about Christ in His eternal kingdom, "showing the great blessing that will attend the millennial reign of the Lord Jesus."[14]

Christ's reign will be a reign of peace. God had said to David, "Behold, a son shall be born to you, who shall be a man of rest; and I will give him rest from all his enemies all around. His name shall be Solomon, for I will give peace and quietness to Israel in his days."[15] The name Solomon also "means 'peaceableness,' for he is a type of Christ reigning in the millennium, after His warfare (typified in David's history) has subdued all enemies."[16] Additionally, David had described the temple as both a "house of rest" and a "footstool of our God."[17] His words "rest" and "footstool" elicit the thought of repose and peace after a victory has been won.

---

13. Ps. 72:2, 4, 7

14. L. M. Grant, *The Psalms*.

15. 1 Chron. 22:9

16. Grant, *The Psalms*.

17. 1 Chron. 28:2

The peaceful reign of Solomon came out of the warfare, labor, and preparation from David's days. In other words, Solomon lived out the good that came from David's reign. When Solomon prayed that God's "promise to David [would] be established,"[18] it meant that he didn't seek to do anything new or to get a new promise from God. He simply fulfilled everything that had been prepared before him. He brought to manifestation all the planning and purpose that had been set before him.

This is how it will be in that day when Christ returns. All of the labor of this age, all of the tears, all of the fighting for God's kingdom will come together and bring in a peaceful reign. All of the preparation that Christ and His church carried out will culminate in a glorious victory. It is a marvelous thought that what we do for God's kingdom today contributes to the glory of that day. It will all add up to the moment when the purpose that God has made known to us will finally be established. We will no longer only believe His promises. We will see those promises established. We will live in the good of them.

A further study of Solomon's name reveals that it comes from the Hebrew word, shalam, meaning "complete, sound, safe, or secure."[19] In fact, this same word shalam is used when talking about the temple finally being "complete" or "finished" in 1 Kings 7:51 and 9:25. We

---

18. 2 Chron. 1:9

19. Francis Brown, S.R. Driver, and Charles A. Briggs, *The Brown-Driver-Briggs Hebrew and English Lexicon.*

are looking forward to a day when everything will be complete. No future tasks will remain to be done. No open projects will yet need to be closed. No more stones will remain to be laid, no more images will remain to be chiseled out, not a single blow of the hammer will remain to be struck. Everything will be done, and everything will be in its perfect, final state.

A Call to Be Like David

What kind of person initiated, planned, and prepared a way for God's dwelling with His people to be established on the earth? It was someone who trusted in God's mercy and threw himself into God's arms at his lowest points. It was someone who accepted God's decision that another man would finish his work. It was someone so empty that he was still able to be filled up with the preparation of the house of God. It was someone in tune with God's current speaking and who listened as the Spirit revealed detail after detail after detail. It was someone who loved God and came to love this house that he was preparing. It was someone who cared for the generations after him and saw beyond his own lifetime. It was someone who would have been filled with an unutterable joy had he been able to live in God's house himself.

David shows us what kind of person was required for God's dwelling place to become solid, glorious, and a testimony to all the world. May we also desire to become people who throw ourselves upon God's mercy, are attuned to the Spirit, and see beyond our lifetime. But how can we develop more into people like David? Perhaps some points in this book thus far have spoken to your heart. I encourage you to dwell on them before the Lord while watching and waiting to see them worked out in your own life. Otherwise, I will end with three things that we can do today that bring us closer to the kind of life that David lived and the kind of person he became.

Grow as Sons

David didn't just help God work on His house. He also allowed God to work *in him*. Even in his last years as king, David was still learning to follow God. He still needed to go through discipline and struggles that fine-tuned his sensitivity to God and taught him God's mind and heart.

Likewise, there is a need for us to grow and develop. T. Austin Sparks has a chapter in his book *God's Spiritual House* that addresses our need to grow as sons. We know that we are sons of God who have been brought into God's house. We've "received the Spirit of adoption by whom we cry out, 'Abba, Father.'"[1] Although being sons in God's house is a fact with "present spiritual meaning" and "something which has to be realized in a spiritual way now," the manifestation and fullness of our sonship "lies in the future."[2] We're still looking

1. Rom. 8:15

2. T. Austin Sparks, *God's Spiritual House*, 14.

forward to the fullness of our sonship, and today we must put ourselves in a position to grow, to come into maturity as sons. Sparks references the following passage from Hebrews:

> And you have forgotten the exhortation which speaks to you as to sons:
>
> "My son, do not despise the chastening of the Lord,
>
> Nor be discouraged when you are rebuked by Him;
>
> For whom the Lord loves He chastens,
>
> And scourges every son whom He receives."
>
> If you endure chastening, God deals with you as with sons; for what son is there whom a father does not chasten? But if you are without chastening, of which all have become partakers, then you are illegitimate and not sons. Furthermore, we have had human fathers who corrected us, and we paid them respect. Shall we not much more readily be in subjection to the Father of spirits and live? For they indeed for a few days chastened us as seemed best to them, but He for our profit, that we may be partakers of His holiness. Now no chastening seems to be joyful for the present, but painful; nevertheless, afterward it yields the peaceable fruit of righteousness to those who have been trained by it.[3]

Sparks points out the word "if"—"*if* you endure chastening, God deals with you as sons." There is still an "if," there is still something waiting to be seen, there is still a chance for us to act upon something.

---

3. Heb. 12:5–11

David allowed himself to "endure chastening" from God. He put himself in the prime position to grow as a son of God rather than flee out from under God's hand. In contrast to David, the Israelites who saw God on the mountain in Exodus did not become the house that God had intended. They "perished in the wilderness. They did not suffer chastening. They would not let God deal with them as with sons... They did not come to their adoption as sons."[4]

This word *chastening* "is confused in our minds with punishing" when "it means nothing of the kind." Sparks, likely referencing the Hebrew 12 verses about fathers correcting their sons, says that "the true meaning [behind *chastening*] is child-training."[5] In other words, if we are to become full-grown sons, today we must put ourselves in a place to be treated as sons under the hand of our Father.

The question seems to be, will we choose to act like children of God or will we live our lives as if we are not? To come into fullness of sons is not a matter of living a perfect life or becoming a powerful Christian. But rather, when God points out a sin in our lives, do we stay with Him, let Him show us the full extent of our darkness, repent, and experience God's mercy? Or do we flee from Him because we want to appear faultless by our own merit? By another example, when God asks us to give up something for Him, something so close to our heart it feels like we would have to rip out a part of it, do we obey and take God's grace even with tears, or run away to avoid His difficult speaking?

---

4. Sparks, *God's Spiritual House*, 14.

5. Sparks, 15.

David was not a son in God's eyes because he was strong and made no mistakes. He was a son because he relied on God alone, acknowledged every mistake, and was put in position after position where only grace and mercy from God could bring him forward. Let us not look down on how difficult it is to live a life like this.

These verses should not make us question whether we will lose or keep our salvation. This is not a matter of losing the love of God. Our salvation is secure, and our adoption can't be revoked. Nothing can separate us from the love of God.[6] But the matter that the Bible presents before us today is whether or not we will come into maturity in our Christian life, and that is very wrapped up in us allowing ourselves to be under the hand of our Father.

Hope for the House of God

David didn't just carry out a mission. His entire heart and being longed for this house that he was building. His hope for the house of God fueled his desire to prepare despite the barriers that were put before him.

Just like David's latter days were full of preparing the stones, wood, gold, silver, and other materials for the building, in a similar way "we are simply quarrying stones out in the mountains and hewing timbers for a building that will be erected by and by when Christ

---

6. See Rom. 8:38-39

Himself shall come and rear a temple for the millennial age."[7] However, David's hope for the house of God infused his actions with a certain purity. Everything he did was for that final goal. Any personal ambitions he had, any personal stores of treasure, were all given in view of that final product.

If we also live our lives by a hope of Christ's return, of the kingdom that we will one day see, we too will have a certain kind of purity in our lives, "content to work at the rough materials, to see our ambitions dissolved and fail, and look forward to the 'future' which David saw, when all our hopes will be fulfilled and we shall dwell in a 'city with foundations, whose architect and builder is God.'"[8] What a purity we have when we build the house *while looking forward to the house*. We don't pay too much attention to any particular stone or timber, as if they are the end in themselves. But each piece is evaluated for the ultimate goal of being fit into the house. If a certain piece does not fit, even if we chiseled at it for hours, we will discard it without hesitation, because our aim is not that one piece but *the whole house*.

May we, like David, have hope for that house that we yet only see in part. "Beloved, ... it has not yet been revealed what we shall be, but we know that when He is revealed, we shall be like Him, for we shall see Him as He is. And everyone who has this hope in Him purifies himself, just as He is pure."[9] These verses make sense.

---

7. Simpson, *Christ in the Bible*, 362.

8. Simpson, *Christ in the Bible*, 362.

9. 1 John 3:2–3

"Everyone who has this hope purifies himself, just as He is pure." If we ultimately hope for that day when Christ will come to claim His church for Himself, then we will pay little attention to our own worldly or religious ambitions. Everything will be measured against what will be glorified in Christ on that day.

Our whole focus and standard becomes what Christ would desire to see. What will He think about me when He comes to claim His church? How will He regard what I am currently putting my hands to? How does my serving today contribute to that amazing outcome we are all waiting for? Watchman Nee has a very good stanza in one of his hymns:

> Unto the judgment seat of Christ
> I daily look away
> May all my living and my work
> Abide the fire that day.[10]

Watchman Nee had a forward-looking attitude even as he was serving God in the day-to-day. These lines do not speak of a need to accomplish a lot for God. I went through a season where I had a constant low-grade fear of not doing enough for Him. But a constant striving to do a lot is not where God wants us to be. Even Watchman Nee, who today benefits so many Christians through his writings, was exiled from the church for a period of time, outwardly unable to do much for Him, but inwardly submitting to Him. Similarly, for a while, the only

---

10. From "What Comfort I Could Feel Anon"

thing David could do was flee from King Saul. He could do little for the kingdom at that time, but he submitted to God in his situation. Perhaps even at that time, what David had in view was not his own kingship, which he could have achieved easily by his own hand, but the ultimate kingship of his Lord.

May we also carry this attitude, hoping for that glorious day when our labor and prayers for the house of God will be fulfilled, realizing that the valuation of our lives is not on how much we do, but how much is done with that same pure hope that David had, desiring to see God get His house and yearning for that day when mankind will be able to dwell fully with their God.

Serve in the House of God

At a certain point, the talk has to be carried out. At a certain point, David had to stop only hoping and dreaming and learning about the temple and start to take action for it. And at a certain point, you will have to stop reading this book and, calmly upheld by God's Spirit within you, figure out what exactly to do to participate in the house of God.

One of David's final ordinances as king changed my perspective about the way I serve in the house of God:

> For David said, "The Lord God of Israel has given rest to His people, that they may dwell in Jerusalem forever"; and also to the Levites, "They shall no longer carry the tabernacle, or any of the articles for its service." For by the last words of David the Levites were

numbered from twenty years old and above; because their duty was to help the sons of Aaron in the service of the house of the Lord, in the courts and in the chambers, in the purifying of all holy things and the work of the service of the house of God, both with the showbread and the fine flour for the grain offering, with the unleavened cakes and what is baked in the pan, with what is mixed and with all kinds of measures and sizes; to stand every morning to thank and praise the Lord, and likewise at evening; and at every presentation of a burnt offering to the Lord on the Sabbaths and on the New Moons and on the set feasts, by number according to the ordinance governing them, regularly before the Lord; and that they should attend to the needs of the tabernacle of meeting, the needs of the holy place, and the needs of the sons of Aaron their brethren in the work of the house of the Lord.[11]

Before David passed the kingdom off to Solomon, he made one interesting decision. Before this point, all the Levites who served in the house of God were numbered from thirty years and above.[12] After peace came to the land, David changed the age to twenty years and above.

When I read this, I did not take the age of twenty and above as some hard and fast rule. Instead, it spoke to me that those who feel young can serve in the house of God. It spoke of a special portion of serving in the house of God that is possible during our young years. It

---

11. 1 Chron. 23:25–32

12. See 1 Chronicles 23:27. Originally instituted by Moses (see Numbers 4:1–3), although the minimum age was lowered to twenty-five at one point (see Numbers 8:23–24).

is because "the Lord God of Israel has given rest to His people." Because Christ has given rest to His people today, even in our early years of knowing Him, we can serve Him. Just like those who have been following God for decades, we get a measure of grace to serve His house too. "It was an honour as well as a duty, and so one can conceive grace acting in calling in the younger men."[13]

The duty of these younger Levites was to "help the sons of Aaron." I took the sons of Aaron to be any older Christian who is putting themselves in to serve the house of God. I wanted to find someone who is crazy for the house of God, who cares for even the tiniest detail of the house of God, who gives their whole life for the house of God. And I wanted to put myself with them as much as I could.

Also, it became clear: it didn't matter what I did in my life, as in whether God called me to get a job or to go into full-time Christian service. My objective was the same either way. Wherever the house of God was, I would be there too. Whoever was serving the house of God, I would be with them.

Through God speaking directly to my heart, these verses created within me a certain commitment to God's house: "Whatever God's house looks like around you, whoever is putting themselves into God's house, put yourself in there and with them. Find Christians who are coming together as God's house and see what you can do there. Find older Christians who are serving in God's house and learn from them. It doesn't matter if it doesn't look the way you hope. That will

---

13. Kelly, *William Kelly Commentary*.

all get worked out. Just be all in. Help in 'the courts and the chambers,' help in 'the purifying of all holy things,' help with 'the showbread and the grain offering,' help with 'what is baked in the pan.' Stand every morning to thank and praise the Lord, stand every evening to thank and praise Him, and at the burnt offerings, and the Sabbaths, and the New Moons, and all the feasts. Attend to the needs of the tabernacle of meeting, and to the needs of the holy place, and to the needs of the sons of Aaron in the work of the house of the Lord."

I didn't know the meaning behind every task listed in these verses, but they showed me that there is so much to participate in in God's house. And what makes our service even sweeter is that we commune with God as we serve. As we serve in His house, we are also dwelling with Him. As we are bearing the responsibility of the Holy Place, we are also singing. As we are going out into the court to help people offer sacrifices to God, we are also entering into the deepest room, where the presence of God waits, eager and joyful to receive us.

In Ezekiel 44, God did not allow the Levites who sinned against Him to minister to Him. Because they had previously worshiped idols, they could not "come near [God] to minister to [Him] as priest, nor come near any of [His] holy things," but they had to "bear their shame and their abominations which they have committed."[14] And yet, God still made them "keep charge of the temple, for all its work, and for all that has to be done in it."[15]

---

14. Ezek. 44:13
15. Ezek. 44:14

I am so thankful that, today, this is not our lot in God's house. How dry it would be to have to serve in God's temple but never approach Him or minister to Him. Yet, I often find that I put myself in that situation, plugging along to fulfill my duty, forgetting that God is right there in the Holiest Place, or even thinking I have no right to enter the Holiest Place.

But we are not like those Levites who had to bear their own shame. Jesus Christ has borne our shame for us, and because of Him we are free to approach God and serve Him with joy, with singing, and even while dwelling with Him. What grace that we can participate in the house in this way! May each of us feel the joy, affection, and hope that King David felt as he prepared for the house of his God, and may each of us, no matter how young or old, new or experienced, feel the calling of Christ as our true King, drawing back the curtains to the sanctuary of the temple, and saying within each of our hearts, "I've given you a place here, too."

Acknowledgements

I'd like to thank Timothy Miller, Sam Faulk, Esther Faulk, and Sarah Watkins for conversations that stirred up consideration of many aspects of King David's life and inspired or developed a number of points in this book. I'd also like to thank Sam Kuo and Kurt Sheu for feedback in the editing stage, as well as Ken Godshall and John Boughan for feedback in the proofreading stage. And finally I'd like to thank my husband Austin for encouraging me during the production of this book, during which an unpractically-minded person like me needs a lot of encouragement.

Bibliography

Augustine. *City of God*. Translated by Marcus Dods. Moscow: Roman Roads Media, 2015. Ebook.

Augustine. *City of God*. Translated by Gerald G. Walsh, et. al. Abridged by Vernon J. Bourke. New York: Image Books, 1958.

Benson, Joseph. *Bible Commentary*. Carlton & Phillips. Bible Hub.

Brown, Francis, Driver, S. R., Briggs, Charles A. *The Brown-Driver-Briggs Hebrew and English Lexicon*. Oxford: Clarendon Press, 1906.

Coates, C. A. *The House of God*. Chessington: Bible and Gospel Trust, 2020.

Darby, J. N. *Synopsis of the Books of the Bible*. Stempublishing.com.

Ellicott, C. J. *Commentary for English Readers*. London: Cassell. Bible Hub.

Grant, L. M. *The Psalms*. Stempublishing.com.

Keil, C. F., Delitzsch, F. *Biblical Commentary on the Old Testament*. Chicago: Phillips & Hunt, 1907. Bible Hub.

Kelly, William. *William Kelly Commentary*. Stempublishing.com.

Nee, Watchman. *The Normal Christian Life*. Carol Stream: Tyndale House Publishers, 1997.

Simpson, A. B. *The Christ in the Bible Commentary, Volume Two*. Camp Hill: Wing Spread Publishers, 2009.

Sparks, T. Austin. *God's Spiritual House.* Originally printed in "A Witness and a Testimony" (1941-1942). Reprinted in *God's Spiritual House*, 2013.

Strong, James. *The Exhaustive Concordance of the Bible*. New York: Eaton & Mains, 1890. Bible Hub.

Made in the USA
Las Vegas, NV
17 November 2024